I WOULD RATHER GO BLIND

T. Jumpi Ete

BLUEROSE PUBLISHERS
India | U.K.

Copyright © T.Jumpi Ete 2024

All rights reserved by the author. No part of this publication may be reproduced, stored in a retrieval system or transmitted in any form or by any means, electronic, mechanical, photocopying, recording or otherwise, without the prior permission of the author. Although every precaution has been taken to verify the accuracy of the information contained herein, the publisher assumes no responsibility for any errors or omissions. No liability is assumed for damages that may result from the use of information contained within.

BlueRose Publishers takes no responsibility for any damages, losses, or liabilities that may arise from the use or misuse of the information, products, or services provided in this publication.

For permissions requests or inquiries regarding this publication, please contact:

BLUEROSE PUBLISHERS
www.BlueRoseONE.com
info@bluerosepublishers.com
+91 8882 898 898
+4407342408967

ISBN: 978-93-6452-221-2

Cover design: Rishav Rai
Typesetting: Rohit

First Edition: June 2024

Acknowledgement

Firstly I would like to acknowledge the extraordinary debt I own to the 13th years old me, thank you for believing in the future you, I will try my best to be where you wished to be. Secondly, I would like to express my special thanks of gratitude to my favorite girl, the very first fan of mine, +and to all my friends, whether I become big or not, even though our paths decide not to meet in future for whatever reason, I want you to know that I will always, be thankful for the support, excitement and believe, you all had shown for my poems, every little words of appreciation and believe, helped me to push myself little by little and my gratitude is here to never die.

And surly not forgetting my mother for her support, my future readers and everyone who has been reading my poem, I would like to thank all of you for your presents in my poetic life.

To my mother, with love

And to all those, once died selflessly with hope for love.

Contents

Light me a little 2
Antique letters 14
Dear rain, ... 34
"If love had a face I would rather go blind" 48
It started as it had to end 76
To, My Lady 82
Wedding bells 94

I WOULD RATHER GO BLIND

Light me a little

"If I don't have myself, Today
The world might not have me Tomorrow"

I killed myself
I saw myself bleeding
But, it was not red
I found what had killed me
It was not a knife, rope or the edge of a roof
But 'I' with thoughts filled by others.

If I ever have the chance
I'll ask, why?
You chose words that drove me to death,
You might argue your innocence
Calming no blood on your hands
But, when your hands will order curfew to your breath
You will know, how words let you kill yourself.

I'm living in a house, I'm never home
Don't ask me why?
Reminds me of peace, I never got to feel.

I'm who creates the darkest shadow
never let the sun reach
but who's gonna tell them
mirror is what they need.

My mother talked me to death
yet showed no remorse
Rather, blamed to be born.
And when did I failed to be a daughter
I guess the day you failed to be father.

They want me to understand but refuse to do so
Talk nothing but sweet
That's what they expect from me
Forgetting their harsh words break me towards the hell.

Where can I find peace, when I can't find it within me.

Don't ask me about the story
Behind my poems
Don't remind me of the misery
I have locked in papers
They try to let go of the spring
My eyes had held for so long
And it can't be stopped, until
It dries on its own
And it's too long.

Who among those stars, looked back
To tell what happens after death.
Who said there is a "7 min" after death?
Who narrated the existence of hell and heaven?
Who saw the burning people?
Who witness the heavenly life?
Who came to tell what's sin enough and what is not.
Who? Made all the alive, decide
Heaven is the best, after life.

If sound doesn't play with those --- never heard
Colors doesn't bother the eyes, once covered in dark
If the songs are not sang by voice ---- unheard
Immortality in heaven ---- must be ater truth.

"It's not dream enough"

It's not dream enough,
If people around you
doesn't laugh about it,
Calling it impossible or
Tell you to come out to the real world.

It's not dream enough,
If your eyes doesn't pour
An unstoppable river,
Your body doesn't freeze out of fear,
For not Giving your best,
if, Everyday doesn't feel like the last chance ,
it's not dream enough,

It's not dream enough,
if you don't work for it,
if your discipline doesn't allow
to follow your rules,
if you don't stretch yourself enough to discomfort,
you are not worthy enough, to dream.

Light up the dark, blow the clouds
Show me the sky
Filled with stars and the moon light
Just for tonight
Let us stand on the roof and pretend
We can fly.

My whimpering heart wander
On the edge of silence
Louder than city – life
Prettier than city – night
Shattered like the stars
Still, find its way to shine
Just like the moon light.

When I look above the line
I see happiness in their eyes,
I wish I had in mine.

All the ink on the palm of my hand
Please, start to rain, as I wish for rainbows
To be the end.

"Don't remember me"

If, I lose myself on the hands of devil
In search for peace, please forgive me!
Maybe, I'm meant to be weak.
However, brave enough to make myself bleed.

If that ever happens,

Don't remember me as a failure
Remember me as an ambitious girl – once lived.
Don't remember the bad – side of me,
Remember me for the smile.
Don't remember me as a girl – failed to succeed
Just remember me as a poet
Died before her poetry.

It's dark and might even get darker
So run as fast as you can
It will be painful, because u will get hurt
Yet still you must run
Before the flash gets down
And it gets dark ---- forever
With nothing but yourself to be, blame.

Antique letters

1811

In the early 18th century, there was a girl called Rain. She was a kind of person, who did not care what people have to say, she always had a respect for her believes and from which, one was for her to be a poet, but back in days, a poem written by a female writer were ignored. "Girls are not suppose to write, let the words play in your heart, don't let it out" was something her mother would always tell her with a sweet voice.

She liked unique and beautiful things that would make her eyes follow. "If a person or a thing you call beautiful, doesn't make your eyes go blind for the world except for the one, it is not beautiful enough" that's what she would always tell her friend, Cecil.

Cecil was a complete different person; he was quite a people pleaser, he care what people have to say, he always chose to believe what majorities believed rather then what he believe. That is why whenever Rain gets irk by him, she would say, "suits your name".

Cecil and Rain met each other in 1809, Rain was new in the town, and Cecil was the one who came to her first and they became very good friends, thanks to Cecil's effort. Everyone in the town thought both of them were soon to be a married couple, who loved each other, because they would always be together. But there was someone no one knew about. A girl called Aline.

Aline was a beautiful women but not many knew about her, because she lived a little far from the town, not many people from the town would go that way. Cecil found that place while they were trying to find a place to hide, where people from town would not bother them, and that is when they met Aline, She was as bright as her name and she was quite a shy girl, but they became very good friends, again thanks to Cecil's effort.

Aline was a 16 year old when she met both 15 year old Rain and Cecil for the first time, they stayed as friends for a long time; however, everything changed on 11th November 1821, when Cecil got married.

1899

When a girl was cleaning her grandfather's room, she found an old box, when she opened the box; she found a little burned and old letters inside, she smiled while reading and asked, "Is this yours." He smiled with tears on his eyes and said "no, your grandmother's." She could not understand but did not say a word, he said, "There is a reason why your name is Aline."

11/04/1811

Letter to the one i love

I hate your eyes, the way it's being polite
Hate the way you smile
Makes me giggle every time
Please, don't bring that smile
If you are not going to be mine, Trust me
it gives me a hard – time
When truth bang on my heart
To tell, I'm not the one
Yet how I wish I were.
I know such kind of things only happens In books
So, I'll just write a letter for you
To know, I exist
With a heart full of you,
I hope this letter finds you well.

11/07/1811

A conversation

Shhh! Tell nobody, Keep this a secret
If heaven knew she exist
They will take her away from me.
"She is not yours or I will rather say
She can never be yours," he said.
She might not be mine Cecil
But in my eyes.
"In this world full of normal, they call it a sin" he replied.
If looking at her with love
Is a merciless death, I would die every day
"And burn in hell" he said it with a displeasure face.
I would rather burn in hell
Playing her image like music in my heart,
Then to Live in peace and continue on to heaven
Forgetting about her.

11/11/1821

I have a story that can't be told
A story that is engraved in me, a story
So sad that I can't stop my tears as I think about it,
Yet so beautiful that I can give up what it is to relive.

11/11/1821

I could hear my heart – beat
In silence, filled with crowd, fear of getting caught
Couldn't resist my eyes
From irresistible you.

11/11/1813

They call my choice weird,
Not because I said
"I like the night"
But, the night without moon
Street without lights
Alley like and evening shadow
And the stars being
The star of the night
Is how I like my Night.

11/01/1815

Her eyes have the voice of beauty
That whispers my name.
When I witnessed her smile
---- For the first time ----
I felt, what "pleasant on the eyes" meant.

11/10/1816

Falling in love with you
Is like falling in love with the flowers
Maybe, not very romantically
But surely, deeply and purely
I bow down with all the love I have for you.

I can never say, "I want you to walk with me"
But every time I feel like my soul died
A little tonight
I walk to you and feel life a little better than last night

11/09/1819

In this world of "Normal"
Said by those who believe
In their false superiority,
I chose to love the beauty.
The kind of beauty
That is sin for those with muddy eyes.

11/06/1820

Letter to the one i still love

I believe you know and if you do not
I hope this letter finds you well

Today, it's been a decade
Since I fell for you
But here my heart remains the same

Every time when I think of you
I pretend to love someone new
I'm not myself, I become someone new
When I think of you.

Every sublime word about love
I might say taking someone else's name
But it was and will always be for you.

Shamelessly, helplessly but hopefully
I write to the one I still love.

All this years that I have loved you, its time you love me too

11/12/1816

Should I ask death --- for you?
Or shall we abandoned life for truth

11/07/1817

I dance, when I hear you sing
Just the thought of us --- for forever
Makes me smile,
Never to float, never to sink, I was meant to drown
With you in my dreams.

11/09/1821

"IF MY VOICE WERE WRITTEN BY MY HEART
LET ME ASK MY DEAREST YOU"

1899

"Why would you marry someone knowing they can never love you back? And why all the letters were written on 11th?"

Instead of being glad to have read her grandmother's letters and surprised or amazed by the fact that her grandmother was once a poet and she didn't knew about it, she was rather confuse, sad and angry. She could not understand the situation, "why do you have to be so selfless and why was she so selfish. If only she refused, you would have married someone who could have loved you for real."

He took a moment before he could reply to her questions; he was lost in his own flashbacks that reminded him, how the prettiest joy and the happiest moment of his life, is also the most painful thing to realize. "What is love?" he asked his grandchild. "To be with the one who will love you the way you do or even more and care for only you," she replied.

"What you just stated, might be right, maybe that's the definition you have for love, but I never had the luxury to think otherwise than my understanding of love. You say, "love is to care" I agree with that, but it's not about how much the other person care for you, but how much you care for the one, despite the fact that the other person might not feel the same. To be able to love someone while accepting the other person's heart with respect, even when it's not you therein. To sacrifice "I" for the one, to be happy for his or her happiness, to love someone with no condition, expectation, desire or possession is something that I have known since I felt love. However, there is one thing I know for sure, because I believe it, "love only happens for once." I had mine and I married her, I must be the lucky one, don't you think."

His words were like heavy weight, sitting on his voice. He continued.

"She was never selfish, she accepted my proposal, because I wanted to marry her, I told my parents that she is the one, I want as my spouse, and they agreed, and talked to her parents and of course they were happy to accept our proposal.

Because her parents liked Me., but I thought, Rain would disagree, but to my surprise, she didn't. I was scared to face her, so I avoided meeting her, until one day she came to me, And asked, "Is this want you truly want" I didn't take a moment to say "Yes". I couldn't see her eye to eye, I was scared of the disappointment her face might have, but when I looked at her, she smiled. I still don't know why, but I never asked.

I know you are wondering why, I wanted to marry her. You see, we lived in a very small town, even if you whisper, next day it's the News of the town. And I knew people were catching on her feelings, and I never wanted the very obvious things to happen to her."

Aline was left with no words, not that she didn't had questions, it's just that she knew it is better not to ask, but there was one thing she couldn't ignore, so, she asked again, " but why all the letters were written on 11th and what happed to your friend Aline?"

"She just disappeared, we both didn't know where she went, the last time we saw her was on our wedding. And about, the letters on 11th. I know nothing about it, I myself wonder but never got to know, I never ask her and she never got the chance to know that I have those letters with me, because she thought she burn them all, but the box she threw into the burning woods never wanted her letters to die"

After hearing her grandfather, she knew one thing for sure; neither of them got their happy ending. She hug her grandfather and said, "you're "The Man" everyone dream of, my dear gentleman".

After Aline left the room, Cecil walked slowly towards his bed and sat on the floor, pulled out an old briefcase, opened the briefcase and took out some old looking papers and went back to his chair, he was happy while looking at the papers, as it was the letters written by him.

"It's been years, my dear"

Dear rain,

03/10/1809

Dear Rain,

Today, it has been a week; since we became friends, but it has been a month since, my eyes knew the existence of your irresistible beauty. I wanted to talk to you since the very first time, but every time my feet tried to move towards you, my heart forget how to breathe, and it is still the same or maybe worst.

The more I get to know about you, the more I realize "Rain is as pure as her name", your face is prettier than the honey shinning beneath the sun.

There is something about your eyes, makes me feel like my heart is falling from a cliff of a never-ending mountain, fall feel as slow as honey to a jar, from a jar, and it never breaks, because you never allow me to touch the ground.

You look heavenly when you smile, it's as if you are smiling for someone to fall for you, I wonder whom you smile for, is it because you are with me or it's a blessing from a lover once lived.

The colour of your hair, enhance the ocean waves hair of yours, I guess your hair died in the most expensive coffee, to be found, only in heaven.

Your skin is soft and smooth like a one year old, even a peach looks like a rotten version of your skin. Your beauty reminds me of the most beautiful summer evening.

26/08/1809

Today I saw a girl; I heard she is new in town. She is the prettiest thing I have ever seen, I felt what I have never felt before, I think she is here to break my heart or maybe she is "The One"

Dear, unknown
Your face easily fit in
The one stayed for years--- faded,
No clues to be seen
Like, it was never a thing.

Did she mean nothing?
Or it's just that "we are meant to be"
Well, I'm wandering in my wonder
Will you ever fall for me?
Or it will be a story
That ends with only me.

30/12/1809

My she, has daisy eyes
Her voice brings rain to desert

My she is lily of the valley
Her smile doesn't hold pride for beauty
Rather bow with sincerity,
But speak of disloyalty can bring fatality

My she, is the words I sing
As I pen my poetry for Immortality.

01/06/1810

Dear Rain,

Today, I heard the rumors about us that have been going ground in the town; I got worried, not about what other has to say about me, but you. I am scared of what they are capable of babbling, I am scared, that you might not be able to take it, and I am scared, that you might end us.

"I can see bushes with covetous eyes
Landing towards us;
Pleasant by the beauty
They try finding flaws, if not,
They make blemish by false."

20/07/1810

Dear Rain,
Now we don't have to worry about people talking about us, because I have found a place for us, Far from people.

"Far away from my town
There is a place, I have found
We can dance to our songs,

Far away, there is a place
Up the hill, we can build
House we dream."

19/07/1811

Dear Rain,

It is the first time, I don't feel any joy, happiness or excitement, while writing for you, I feel like my soul left my body, I'm like a breathing corpse. I can't accept, I don't want to..

Don't take me as a person who despise that kind, but try asking my pain, you will know the depth of the wound you have left by herein , it was so easy for you to show your love for her, in front of me, I could hardly hold my tears.

For whom, I stared writing, told me she writes for someone else, it surly hurts, but the fact that there is no way that she would ever be in love me, is want hurts the most.

I think, this is going to be the last letter, from me to you.

- *Finis*

12/12/1816

Dear Rain,
I guess, I can never stop writing, when it comes to you. I thought you not liking the "I" that I projected, hurts the most, but I was wrong. Not being able to see the smiling face of yours, not being able to witness the happy you, pain me the most.

Wind passes by touching you, I breath.
Every road you walk through
Tells me to follow you.

When shadows of sorrow rain on you
You let your night tears flow,
Slowly, it starts to rain on my mind,
I can't stop myself from looking at your window
Through mine, just to see if you are all right and
Like always, I end up sitting by my window
Talking to myself,

"Will you smile, if I tell you, what's in my notes for you?"

12/12/1816

Beauty failed to hide the pain
Pain couldn't cover beauty.

The saddest beauty I have ever seen,
The Deepest pain --- ever --- was felt by me

How much pain she has buried inside
I wonder while wandering her beautiful side

17/09/1819

Dear Rain,

It's the second letter, after I wrote, *"I think, this is going to be the last letter, from me to you"*

Today, I want to confess, confess about how, I started hating you for not liking me, and to break my dreams, dreams where we were happy together, building our home, just you and I, I was in my own delusion and I couldn't take it, when I saw it falling down in a blink of an eye.

I'm sorry, for all those time I was being rude, I know I became someone I shouldn't have , I know you were hurt, but you never let me go, even though you were sad, you never let it show, but I became selfish, not realizing the reality.

But, now I know, I can never hate you, I never hated you, to honest, how can I? when I find my happiness in yours, even thought I can't have dreams about you falling in love with me, I can never stop falling for you.

"When you came to me and went away
Like a winter rain,
I could not help but hate
But, with time, everything faded
Except, the sublime side of you."

14/09/1878

Dear Rain,

It's been 5 years, since you left me. Each day feels like a year to pass, I wish death would come to me sooner, than my day. I wonder, will I ever meet you in heaven; will you recognize me, or the two of us will forget about each other.

Now, I realize why, you said, you will rather choose hell than heaven, I feel it now, I'll also rather burn in hell, than to forget about you in heaven.

"Your absence reminds me of those evening
On the rainy days
When clouds stops to rain"

30/10/1899

Dear Rain,
This is my last letter to you, I know, I said this before, but this is really my last one, because I don't think I will live long enough to write you the next one. My hands are shaking as I'm writing, some of my words are not clear enough, but still, I am writing, because I believe in next life and when you are born again, I hope this words finds you well and the "you" get to be with the one you truly love.

Now, as I'm old and grey
You and I are not us anymore
And my hands doesn't work the same
Legs tremble, involuntarily
Zealous for life, disappeared
Like it never meant a thing
And vague memories are the only thing that's left
---- At this autumn age ----
You are the only vivid memory I have
And our indelible story is the only thing
That makes me want to live a little longer.

--- to be continued

"If love had a face

I would rather go blind"

We didn't choose to like each other
It happened, without us knowing,
What we did chose was silence,
Nobody could see or feel
I never tried to have a conversation with you
About how I felt,
Neither did you, because
We both knew
There is a fear insides us
That will never go, but
I would always look your way
Without me realizing,
Only to realize
Our eyes never learn.

To, the one
I chose to let go

"You're like an unnamed season
That comes after winter
Before spring
Just for a moment, but
The best one can ever feel"

To, the one
I choose everyday

You are like the weather
Before storm, I can't decide
Whether to care
for My fear, or just
Stare at the beauty
And let it destroy me.

Wet eyes, waiting in a cold night
Even red wine can't save me tonight
So, light my cigarette, one last time
Warm me up, like the day
We first "collide"

I'm drowning, save me
Before I die
It's cold down here
Pull me up, before I lose my mind

For one last time
Light my cigarette with yours,
Because, even red wine
Can't save me tonight.

The worst is disguise as him
But, she can tell nobody
Nobody believes, because
The truth is disguise as her.

Today, I am too tired to write a poem,
But my heart won't stop
So I will write you a prose about
How we never made it
Because we never started,
Yet we have pages written down on us
I wonder what those were about
I don't remember any of it,
Do you, remember?
I guess it was about the way our eyes met,
Knowing it will never work
Or maybe about how
We wished to be together
Knowing we can never be together
If not, then I guess it was about
The distance we hold
I for you and you for me.
The chapters we both skipped,
I never wish to turn back and read,
Not because I don't want to or I hate it
It's because I will never make it to the end
So I can only wish you a happy goodbye.

I said, I gave it all,
But you say, it was not enough
You said, you did your best
But I say, I never felt!

I gave you the clear sky
Yet you asked for the rain,
And when it started pouring
You said, "I like the autumn better "

You gave the prettiest maple
Yet I was searching for the snowdrops,
And when the whole spring was brought to me
By you, I was looking for a bare tree

Finally, it was summer
We wished for,
But, the ice melted, so did we.
It's not you or I
But us to be blame.

If I tell you, would you understand or just listen
And even if you understand,
Will it change? Will I change?
Will my heart that can't stop but to ask for death,
Before every sleep
Heart that doesn't want to live
Will it change, just because now that you understand

I know if you asked me
About Things I wish you would
Things that I can't say it on my own
Without questions,
I know if you could understand me
Just a little, back then
It would have made me cry
Tears of hope and happiness
Could have made me smile,
"Now" is too late, because
I have cried until my tears ran dry.

What will my heart take, to love you again?
How much of tears for you
To feel what I felt, how much of pain for you
To understand me, How much of love
For you, to love me like once I did.

I'm surely not the moon
You want to talk too
Also, not the sun you hide from
But gladly, I'm the star you can't ignore
While wishing for the moon.

Sometimes, try looking for me
From the darkest mountains
Then you will know,
I look prettier than any version of the moon

Night walk, holding hands, counting stars,
And names on an unknown wall

Stars starts to whisper, it's getting louder
As they do it together

Moon told us to hide, beneath the sun light,
Let the Sun dry up the river, before rain turn the water Muddy.

I'm in love, but
Not with someone in it
I am alone, herein
Yet, I find my joy in my delusion
Sometimes I create my own happy forever.

My friends try to bring me out it
But, I have my own excuse
"I am already with him, he just doesn't know it yet
He make me cry but doesn't realize"
"How would he, when your existence
Is nowhere to be found in his memories" my friend replied.

So, I cried for only a night
Promised my friends "I will never think of him"
But, I guess promises were meant to break.

They think, there is nothing more beautiful,
He is what everyone wishes to have
But, the one who gets to meet
The real self of him
Have a different story to tell.

There was a girl, I liked,
One summer, but my heart denied,
Now, every summer my heart cries,
Calling her name, but now she deny,
That she ever cried.

You are everything I would not choose
Still, I can't stop myself From
Looking at you.

Should I write summer for you?
Or shall I be the winter to you
Though I know --- fall is the truth.

I like you and I don't see anything or anyone else,
My head starts to burn and my body
Starts to warm and shake,
Thoughts fight against each other
"You might love me but never the same"
My love will never be justified
Because they try to distance us,
But, I'll always stay at the very same place
Always ready to hold you.
However, this time, it's your turn to clam.

You have been on my mind
Since I last slept, when was that?
I don't remember, since it was not yesterday

I'm still struggling
As if the day you left was yesterday,
But, when was it?
I don't remember, since it was not yesterday.

"How much you love" --- she asked.
Silence got my answer
How could I tell, when I have so much
But, can't be expressed in words.

They tell me to stay away from you,

"If I am, the poet ---- you are my poetry
If I am, the stylus --- you are the ink that plays the story"

So, being a poet, how am I
Suppose to run away from my poetry.

Do you think of me?
The way I think of you.

Do you count the stars?
The way I count days,
I have spent without you.

Do you look back on me?
The way I do, when
We part our ways apart.

Do you ever look at the mirror?
The way I look at you

Your smile, save it up, for only me
The world doesn't deserve to see,

You were made for me, as I am for you,
But don't tell the world yet
They won't accept me,
I can't blame them
I feel it too --- amusing right?
Yet, I'll say it again, I can feel them,
The pain of not having you,
I felt it --- once in my heart.

Lover, from the past life
I guess, I made you suffer,

Now you are going to suffocate me till I die,

I guess, I made you cry till you died,
Now, you won't let my tears dry,
Before the next cry.

Glasses off and people will see the beauty behind,
But, will the blur, face of you
Will still flatter my heart
Which has already been flattered?

I heard you're in pain
Heard you stand under the rain
To hide all your tears and pain,
No one to hear what you got say,
Thus, that makes you
Miss old radio days.

Do you miss, without knowing?
What you're missing.
Do you fell void surrounding your whole body?
Yet, so full
Do you smile, trying to hide?
You cried.
Do you wish the day to never fall?
Therefore, the night might never rise.
Does midnight caress you to tear?
And dawn remains you the fear

Photographs of you in my secret album
I neither ripped nor burned
Rather arranged in tier, from first to last,
"Redamancy" hah ….foolish of me
To think you had in you ---- for me.

Amateur I, fooled the levity in me
Thus, that helped my truth
To reach the metanoia, toward falsity
But, who am I to victimize my slavery for you
When, I was the one to offer.

It started as it had to
end

"HOW IT STARTED"

Never thought of you or decided to choose you
Until she grabbed my heart with her words
Those were all about you.

It was the night
Moon was bright
We were having girl's night
I was still unknown about
The beginning that night have had for me,
It all started when time reached the silence
As everyone had heavy eyes
Dead but still alive, Living the other side
But she decided to break the curfew that night
And we both became an owl for a night.

Dawn touched our eyes
We couldn't sleep whole night
As she decided to be the narrator for you
And narrated you as a wonder drug
No wonder, how you became
My desire to possess.

I was a spring leaf
Waiting summer to pass
Autumn to start
Just so, I could fall in your arms.

I caught a glimpse of you
On the blossom day, as you entered
Like an autumn leaf
That day, I had no clue
I'll fall for you.

"AS IT ENDS"

The night she broke the curfew
And had me fall for you
Every word my ink played
Had something for you

But, today truth grabbed the rose
Inside my soul, I was hurt
As thorn played its role

I see no clouds, today
Sky look like a lonely place to hide
Today, I don't wish to grab starts
I wish to end the night, before it starts

To, the story I wrote before I cried
Story that made me smile
To the places I went
Looking for his name, to the untamed heart I had
I thank, as it ends.

To,

My Lady

My dear Lady,

"Until its salience and we become the rhythm
To poems of our own, I will keep you in my heart
Safely in silence"

I know, my words don't know how to play Love,
But, how? The eyes of my lady, failed to read mine."

"WHAT IF'
"WHAT IF'
"WHAT IF'
Only if I knew, I will chant "what if "
I would have tried a million times, before
The Goodbye

My dear Lady,

I am the poetry that makes you cry,
The saddest line, in songs
An unforgettable misery
A movie leaves behind,
I am a Mari; I die on ground with muddy grasses and rain,
Never in books.

Tell me,
How to write you a better poetry
---- Than you are

Tell me,
When can I read you the sonnet, once I wrote for you ----
Incomplete,
Yet finished

Tell me,
Before I forget ---- what I ever felt.

Let it whisper through our gaze
Don't say it out loud
It will only destroy
What we have now

"Love is love" maybe just a spell
From another dimension,
If not, why being with thee feels so gay, but
Sounds so wrong.

They tell me to stay away from you,

"If I am, the poet ---- you are my poetry
If I am, the stylus --- you are the ink that plays the story"

So, being a poet, how am I
Suppose to run away from my poetry,
How am I suppose to bleed on papers?
If there is no ink to help my feather.

The ashes of old memories, I hold
Just like the day,
My fear and the comforting you
Got our hands tangled.
Our hands moved on, but my heart
Still live in those 11 seconds of ours.

When did I know, I was in love?
It's funny! How it's so simple
Yet, so hard to explain

I guess it was when my eyes
Were pleasured by your existence,
Or maybe when I was foolishly
Trying my best to find Apricity
In December rain,
If not, then maybe
When I tried to find solution
Out of my delusion, saying
"My lily of the valley will never bring me fatal flaw"
Or maybe, when I thought I can fight against
Those with muddy eyes,
Maybe, maybe
It was the day I first saw you.

Wedding bells

We met again, like the lead characters
in movies, 0n wedding day
The girl I knew and the boy you met
Brought us together
In this hall filled with promises
With hope for love to stay forever
Many died together, many with someone else
Now I was part of this crowed.
However, today is not my day, but one day
you and I out of my dreams

You looked at me and smiled
I looked into your eyes and tried to find, why?
Found nothing, a friend of a friend
just a girl you witness time to time, nothing more
but if you look in mine, you don't even need to try and find
it's shamelessly naked in my eyes.

When I saw you enter, with that black trouser on
and almost white kind of pink shirt, I looked at myself
and wished, you wore that knowing, I'll be in black
this thunder of delusion never stops, it's getting worst
with the sound of wedding bells.

www.ingramcontent.com/pod-product-compliance
Lightning Source LLC
LaVergne TN
LVHW041618070526
838199LV00052B/3194